I0472341

Instagram Growth Secrets

The Ultimate Guide To

Growing A Massive Following Fast & How To

Make Money Along The Way

By Alec Scherger

Printed in the United States of America

First Printing, 2019

ISBN 9781091922457

www.alecscherger.com

Table of Contents

Introduction

This book does NOT guarantee you will grow your following or reach any level of financial success. I do not purport any 'get-rich-quick' schemes, nor do I provide 'simple-steps' to financial freedom. I believe in hard work and consistency. Your results and success are dependent on you.

My name is Alec Scherger aka @alecsugar. I am an entrepreneur from Ohio, and I have a passion for growing niche related Instagram accounts. I started Instagram as a hobby; it was a game to me for see how many followers I could get per month or week. Instagram is very profitable, and you can make a great living at it if you have patience. I will teach you how to grow your Instagram to over 1,000 followers a day and get hundreds of thousands, if not millions of views and likes on your posts. You will also learn the different ways you can make money with Instagram, and how to get advertisement deals with big companies.

There are certain levels to Instagram accounts; once you get them to a certain point or level, you can stop doing some things that you have done before. In this book, I will teach you the things you need to do and not do to grow your following as fast as possible. You can implement these strategies for niche accounts as well as personal accounts.

Follow For Follow

Chapter One
Follow For Follow

Follow for follow is the oldest trick in the book, you are probably thinking; "Alec, this better not be the big secret." No, it is not a secret, but I am telling you that targeting is key, and if you target the right people they will respond to you. ONLY do the follow for follow method if you have less than 3,000 followers.

When using the follow for follow method you follow other accounts hoping they will follow you back; this is one of the most basic methods anyone has ever used. Instagram will know if you are doing the follow for follow method and put you on somewhat of a blacklist, which is okay when your starting out. The only reason it is okay is because when your starting there is no way for anyone to find you except through hashtags, and even then your posts will be at the bottom of the page. Before you might have been using hashtags on your post and it would have gone straight to the bottom of the hashtag page and no one would ever see it. After implementing the method more people will see your posts faster and they will not be at the bottom of the page. Whenever I have used this method I have grown tremendously faster than compared to just using hashtags.

When implementing the follow for follow method you need to target a specific group of people related to your niche. Mass follow personal accounts that like, follow, and comment on niche accounts related to yours. Just remember to keep the follow/unfollow rate below 150 per hour or you will start receiving temporary bans. It will ban you from following and unfollowing people for a few hours or even a day. Go to accounts that are highly active, and target the niche account's audience in hopes that they will follow you back. After you follow them, wait around two to three days before you unfollow, chances are 10-15% will follow you back. Automation is key and I will get into that in more detail in another chapter, but to make the most of your time, automate the follow for follow method.

Remember to use the follow for follow method only if you have less than 3,000 followers. Always use hashtags on your posts even when you are using the method. Also automate the follow for follow method so you don't go crazy and definitely remember to target people that are already interested in the same category of posts as your niche. If you remember these key things the follow for follow method should go smoothly for you.

Chapter Two

Posting

Chapter Two

Posting

In this chapter, I will teach you many things you did not know about Instagram that will skyrocket your engagement, and make many more of your posts go viral (virality is a key step to growth hacking your instagram). This chapter will apply to everyone at all stages of their account.

When you create or pick out your content, one of the ways to maximize your engagement is to make sure the video or picture is in the horizontal position. Posting horizontally not only looks good, but it maximizes the time your followers or potential followers see it. That has two benefits, one being Instagram's algorithm will recognize that and reward you by showing the post to more accounts. The longer an account stays on your post the better! The second reason is; potential followers will see the beautiful content filling up their screen and will be more apt to follow. If you have ever seen a picture that fills up the majority of the screen, it looks amazing; you feel immersed in it!

Post great content and follow trends; do not just post boring content that everyone sees everyday. Instead, look at what trends are floating around and do not be afraid to try new things. When it comes down to it be experimental and use your imagination: Who knows? It might be the next thing to go viral!

Some of the best engaged posts I have had were using Instagram's multiple, picture, posting feature. These types of posts are the best to engage with your followers, to ask them questions, or to tell them to go follow someone or like something. You can put up to 10 pictures or videos on these posts and it can keep followers engaged and on the post for a while. It is very good for companies that have multiple variations of one product and for niche accounts when your advertising for those companies.

When growth hacking your Instagram you want to post very often, about three to four times a day. Although you will see a decline in the engagement of each post, and with all posts combined you will reach far more people than you would have with one to two posts everyday. Another factor for great engagement is posting at a consistent schedule. Post scheduling services like Buffer.com are essential for success on Instagram. It takes about two days of work each month to schedule posts for an account; after that you don't have to worry about posting until the next month.

When you grow a lot of accounts in the same niche, you will only have to schedule one set of posts per niche. This will help you from scheduling 60 different posts for each account everyday which would be crazy. Buffer.com is what I use and it is very simple and lays everything out for you, but it is only for scheduling posts. For an 8 account subscription it is only $15 a month, which is only $1.87 per account per month. So you only will be spending $22.50 dollars a year for each account. If you don't want to schedule posts for each account you can just schedule posts for one account on Buffer.com. Then go over to Gramto.com and use their auto repost tool. You can target your smaller accounts to repost the posts you manually scheduled from your bigger account. The posts will then be reposted to your smaller accounts once your main account (the one you manually scheduled the posts for) posts to its feed. This is a feature that you can set and forget. Just don't forget to schedule your posts for the next month.You can use this model for as many niches and accounts as you want. You could have 100 accounts reposting from your main account if you really wanted too!

(1st Niche) Your biggest and best
Instagram account (Only one)
with scheduled posts from Buffer.com

On Gramto.com use the auto
reposting tool for more
accounts in the same niche

Don't be afraid to follow trends also try new things and innovate. To reach your highest potential followers everyday; always post at least three times a day. Maximize your screen space by using tall content. Use the posting model I use to grow a high volume of accounts. Always use your analytics (or Insights). Remember, the better you understand your audience, the better your account will prosper.

Using Your Analytics

Chapter Three

Using Your Analytics

Using your Insights (or analytics) is a great way to get ahead. When you want to growth hack your Instagram they are your best friend. If you study your analytics you will have a better understanding of your account and know what performs best at what time.

The Insight that is the most crucial is your most active follower times. Posting at the wrong times could decide whether your post does good or terrible.

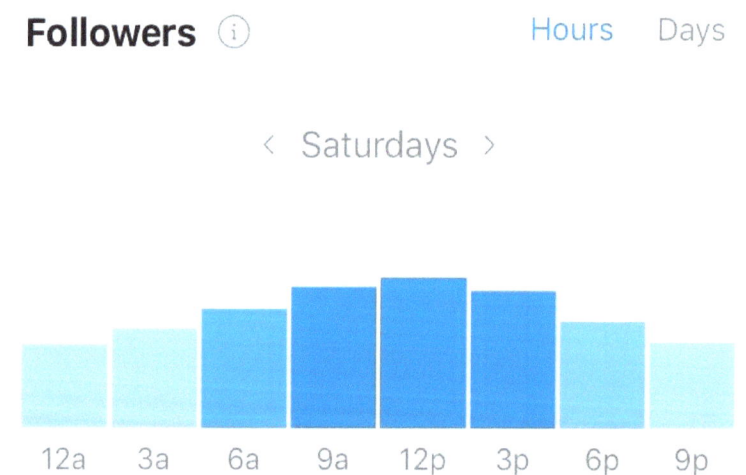

The first 30 minutes of any post is the most crucial; some of the times you can tell if your post will go viral within that first 30 minutes. To tell if your post is going to do good you will notice an increased engagement, rather having the post not initially getting good engagement. Do not get me wrong; I have had times where I thought a post was going to do terrible but it surprised me, and was one of my top performing posts that week.

On Instagram, you can see the Insights for each individual post. Studying your Insights for individual posts will help you get a good idea of what type of content does best. When looking into your individual posts you can see the amount of likes, comments, shares, and saves.

7.3K   146   372   641

If you look at the number of accounts reached, it tells you the number of individual accounts that have seen your post. Instagram will also tell you the percentage of people that are not following you that have seen that post.

Discovery ⓘ

97,513
Accounts reached
83% weren't following you

Under the impressions tab, you will also see the location where people saw your post like home, the explorer page, your profile, and other. These analytics are great to have and will help you understand how your followers respond to certain content you post.

Impressions   108,473

From Hashtags   43,930

From Home   22,274

From Explore   6,557

From Other   35,712

This is where your post was seen the most. It got the most impressions from Hashtags, Home and Explore.

If you want to get more involved with your following analytics, Social Blade is a great way in doing so. With Social Blade, not only can you track the rate of which you gain followers, but the followers rank, following rank, media rank, and engagement rank. These rankings will give you a good idea were you place in the Instagram world, but are not really going to help with growing your account. Social Blade also gives you your engagement rate, average likes, and average comments. They base the engagement rate based off of the last 20 posts on your account and is a good analytic to know, especially if a potential buyer of your account asks you. Your average likes and comments is good to know when you are selling your account and shoutouts. Social Blade is a great, free resource, that lets you in on valuable information to your Instagram account.

Your Story Insights are essential when growing your account. You can use polls, questions and many other things to get peoples opinions; Instagram's stories is great for that. If you were to use a poll in one of your stories, go into the Insights and you can see the viewers, people who clicked "no", and people who clicked "yes".

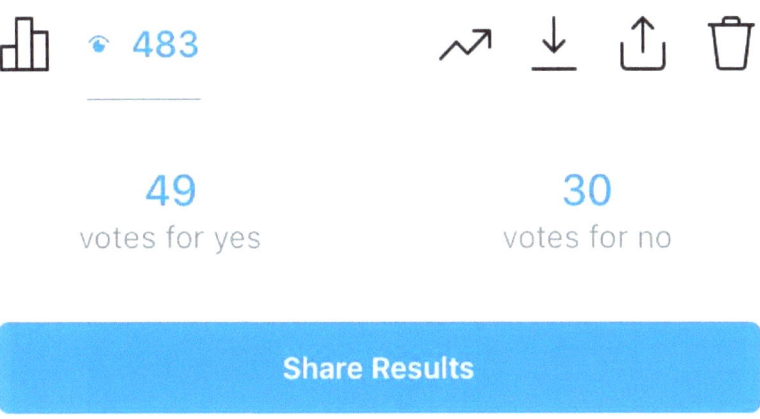

You can also see your impressions, follows from that story, and where the person navigated to after your story. Instagram's story Insights are pretty much straight forward and can be very useful.

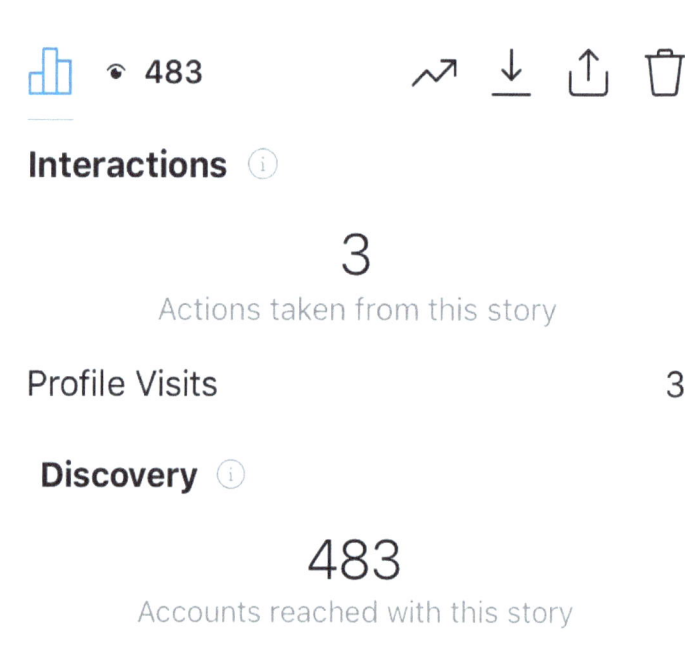

Interactions ⓘ

3

Actions taken from this story

Profile Visits   3

Discovery ⓘ

483

Accounts reached with this story

Impressions   549

Follows   0

Navigation   448

Back   6

Forward   319

Next Story   66

Exited   57

Using your Insights is a great way to get ahead in the Instagram game. Studying your analytics for individual posts can help you get a higher price when selling your account. It will also help you when selling promotions. Using Social Blade is a smart idea and is a great, free resource, to learn about things on your account, that you otherwise could not through Instagram's Insights. Using your Insights is essential when growth hacking your account.

Hashtags

Chapter Four

Hashtags

Hashtags are very simple and are a great source of engagement. A post with at least one hashtag averages 12.6% more engagement than a post without any. You always want to use hashtags whether you are putting them in the actual caption, or in the comments. You can even put your own branded hashtag in your bio so people can follow it. You also will have a better chance at them seeing the post if they follow your hashtag.

It is okay to use the same sets of hashtags in every post. Just make sure those hashtags are relevant to the content your posting. Relevant hashtags will be beneficial to your content growth. It won't hurt your account, but it won't help much to use hashtags that are not related to the post. Remember to not use more than 30 hashtags and you will be all set. Do not overthink it, hashtags are very simple, but powerful if used the correct way.

A post with at least one hashtag, averages 12.6% more engagement than a post without any. Make a set of relevant hashtags, and use them for the majority of your posts. Remember to not use more than 30 hashtags per post. Hashtags are very simple yet powerful at the same time, so do not overthink it.

Chapter Five

Automation

Chapter Five

Automation

Automation is what ties everything in this book together; it is your foundation to success on Instagram. There are many different things that you can automate, from scheduling your posts, to liking others pictures. Automation is key when growing a successful Instagram account. Without automation services you would not be reading this right now because I would not have been successful on Instagram; that is how important this is.

Automating your posts is the most important thing you can do to grow your account fast. Not only will you get posts out at specific times throughout the day, but once you schedule all your posts for the month, you will be relieved that you will not have to worry about it for another 30 days. This is where you need to figure out the best three times of the day to post. Lets say your best posting time is at 12 o'clock PM; I would schedule one at 9:30 AM the second at 10:30 AM and the third at 11:30 AM, that way all of your posts go out right before the most active part of your day. Leave at least an hour between each post so it gives Instagram a time for it to show people each one, instead of posting all three at 11:30 and Instagram showing only one of those posts to everyone.

If you pick the time where the majority of your followers are on Instagram and post a half hour before that, your posts will have a better chance at going viral.

Automate your follow for follow method. This will be a huge burden off your shoulders and you will not always have to be searching for people. You can direct your automated following to follow accounts that follow certain people, hashtags, and like certain pictures. Just like any other automation, you can choose how often the system will follow someone. Try to stick around following 110-130 per hour anymore and you might run into problems with Instagram's algorithm. Target accounts that follow other big accounts like yours; at least two-three of them. Automating the follow for follow method will be a huge help to you by getting you a lot of engaging followers and by saving you a ton of time.

Automating everything after a while can be a burden to your account, so be careful to not automate everything. One thing you should not automate is auto liking, in the beginning it sound great right! Well no, you should not automate it because with Instagram's algorithm it knows how much time you actually spend on Instagram, you need to spend a little time on Instagram acting like a real human. By acting like a real human I mean actually logging into the app, roaming around, and liking some pictures. Instead of the auto poster logging in for less than a minute, just to post and log back out. Spending a little time everyday or every other day liking some pictures will help your account. Instagram's algorithm checks to see if you are acting like a human or a robot. If you just use auto post, never like anyone's pictures, and do not spend any time on Instagram, the algorithm will recognize that as not being human like and may put your account on the backburner. It may not show your posts to all the people it potentially would if you would have been acting like a human. At the end of the day, do not automate everything you possibly can, you will be glad you did not.

Remember to schedule your posts every month so you stay sane. Do not use every automation feature available; you do not want to spam your account. Log into to your account every few days so Instagram senses that your acting like a human. Schedule your posts to publish at the most active times of the day so you can have the best chance for them to go viral. After you automate your Instagram you will be relieved and ready to go onto the next venture. Remember without automation services, you would not be reading this right now because I would not have been successful on Instagram; that is how important this is.

Selling Promotions

Chapter Six
Selling Promotions

There are a few different ways to make money with Instagram. One of those ways is by selling shoutouts. This includes not only shouting out accounts smaller than yours but also advertising products for companies. When selling promotions you can make a pretty good income very fast.

Once your account starts getting good traction (probably to at least 250,000 to 500,000 impressions per week) you will start receiving D.M.'s and emails from companies or smaller accounts wanting you to promote them or their product. If you are not receiving these messages, try putting something like "D.M. for promotions" in your bio. Adding that simple message will show that you are serious about any business inquiries and that you are open to doing business.

You can also search for businesses on Instagram and send them a simple D.M. saying you are willing to promote their products or services for a certain price. Always remember to price your services a little higher than you think. The potential buyer has a perceived value and you need to make that perceived value as high as possible. If you were to charge $10 per shoutout, sure it would be more affordable, but it does not sound like it has a lot of value in it. The $50 shout out sounds like it has a lot more value and will be more attractive to potential customers. You may get less customers with a higher price but would you rather get 20 customers at $10 per post(which is $200), or ten customers at $50 per post(which is $500) and you do not have to do as much work. The bare minimum that you should charge is two dollars for every thousand impressions your posts average. With shoutouts, It looks very professional to create somewhat of an advertisement banner. It helps to promote your advertisement services, and all you need to do is send them to potential clients. You want to be straight to the point, and lay out everything in a basic way.

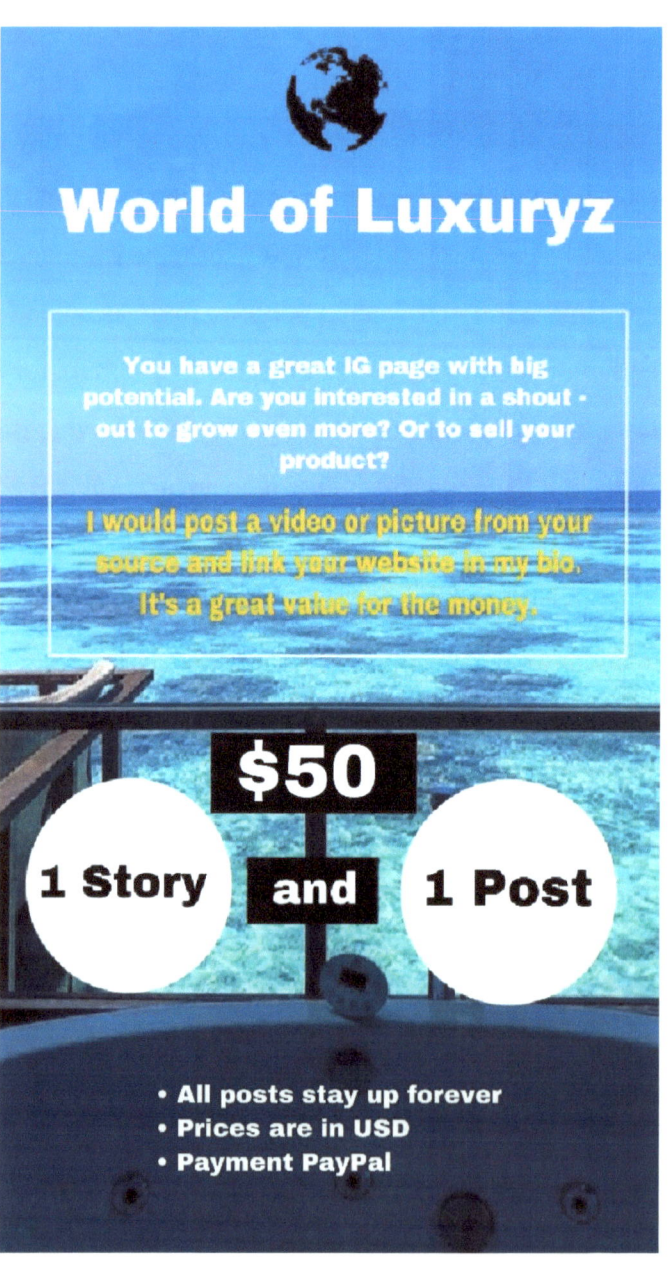

World of Luxuryz

You have a great IG page with big potential. Are you interested in a shout - out to grow even more? Or to sell your product?

I would post a video or picture from your source and link your website in my bio. It's a great value for the money.

$50

1 Story **and** **1 Post**

- All posts stay up forever
- Prices are in USD
- Payment PayPal

After you have sold a few shoutouts, always go back and talk with your customers and ask if the promotion was beneficial to them. Ask them ways they think you can improve your promotions. If they were happy with your service, talk to them after a few weeks and ask if they would like another promotion. If they do not, talk to them a couple weeks later and chances are they will want another promotion. Selling shoutouts certainly won't be where you make most of your money, but you still can make a pretty good side income from it.

Price your shoutouts based on the average amount of impressions you receive per post. Make an advertisement banner displaying your prices with simple guidelines. Remember, potential customers place a perceived value on your services, and you need to make that as high as possible. Make it as high as possible through strategic pricing and a high quality advertisement banner. Always follow up with your customer to see if there is anything you can do to make your service better. Just remember to follow these steps and you will see results.

Growing Accounts To Sell

Chapter Seven
Growing Accounts To Sell

Building and selling Instagram accounts is a great way to make money. Maybe you are reading this book and just want to build accounts as fast as you can to sell them. Building and selling Instagram accounts is a great way to go when you want to make a lot of money.

Assuming you already built your Instagram, and you are ready to sell; you will want two main things: a high amount of followers, and a high rate of engagement. Never sell an Instagram below 100,000 followers, even though it may take you awhile, it will be far worth it in the end. If you had an account with only 90,000 followers the only buyers that would be interested in it are looking for a great deal. The experienced buyers know once you hit 100,000 followers, the value of your account will go up like crazy. Many people when looking to buy accounts, already want lots of followers and a 100,000 following looks a lot better than a 90,000 follower account even when there is a price difference of a few hundred, to even a couple thousand dollars.

What will ultimately determine the price of what you sell your account for is your engagement rate. To make your engagement rate go up, post only once a day, each of your posts should get a higher rate of engagement than if you were posting three times a day to grow your account. Do that for a few weeks before you sell your account, so potential buyers see the higher engagement. Doing that will be more persuasive to the potential buyers of your account and you will be able to charge more. Building and selling Instagram accounts is a great way to go when you want to make a lot of money fast.

Buying accounts and flipping them is another great option. When flipping an Instagram account you buy a lower followed account usually between 25,000 - 65,000 followers and then you grow it substantially more than when you got it and sell it for a profit. When looking for accounts to buy, one option is to look at accounts that have not posted for a while. Usually that means that they do not know what to do with the account or they want to sell it. You usually can get these accounts for the cheapest. Before you buy the account ask the seller to post at least two posts so you can see the engagement rate to tell if it is even worth buying. If you try to buy accounts that are active, chances are they are going to be more expensive. You may have more active followers and will be able to grow faster than an account that is not active.

When making an offer, always start low, you do not want to put down your maximum offer and then have the seller say that it is not high enough. Do not be afraid to walk away; chances are if they really want to sell they will come back to you in a few days. Always outline how the sale will go through before you agree on a price. How are you going to give them the money? Who will exchange first? The safest way to exchange money and accounts is to give the seller 50% of the agreed upon amount then have the seller give you the information to the account. After you login to the Instagram account and email account change the passwords and then give the seller the rest of his or her money. If anything goes wrong, like if the seller scams you (which has happened to me) at least your only out half of the agreed upon amount.

After you bought an Instagram, account you can choose to keep the same name or change it. Preferably you want to keep it the same name, but if you do end up changing it, at least keep it in the same niche. If you do decide to change the name of the account you will notice a drop of followers that may continue for a few months. Eventually it may look like you are growing slowly, but you might just be losing followers while gaining followers at the same time. That will make the follower count grow very slowly.

After that few months, you will be back in the race and be pumped more than ever!

Never sell an Instagram account below 100,000 followers. Make sure you have a high engagement rate before you try to sell your account. It can be even more profitable and faster in some cases if you buy an existing account to flip. When making an offer always start low and do not be afraid to walk away. If you change the name of the Instagram account at least keep it in the same niche. Building and selling Instagram accounts is a great way to go when you want to make a lot of money in the long run.

Affiliate Marketing

Chapter Eight
Affiliate Marketing

If you want to make even more money over a longer period, affiliate marketing is going to be your bread and butter. In this chapter, I will share with you how to get an affiliate marketing deal and how to sell to your audience.

With affiliate marketing you do not make a set amount per post, rather you make a percentage of whatever you sell. Out of these three ways to make money this is where you will make the most money if you do it right. Affiliate marketing is pretty much straight forward, a company will more than likely contact you to be an affiliate marketer for them. When choosing what company to go with, look at their products; do their products fit in the same niche as your account? If so you will need to use content that looks the least like an ad. When you have the words "sale" or just a product and a price in your post they do not do as good as a regular post. Do not use any content that just has a picture of the product and nothing else. You need to create or use somewhat of a lifestyle picture of someone using the product. Also always remember potential customers are far more likely to buy your product if there is a face in the picture because it gives them someone like them to relate to. Then they will be far more likely to remember that product and buy it.

Some of the most popular products on the internet right now are courses. These courses can teach you how to sell on Amazon, dropship, grow your Instagram, and many more. Most of the time these courses are through a prerecorded video that the teacher has made. Selling courses can be a very lucrative business because in some cases these courses can be close to $700 and if you are getting paid 30% that is $210 that you made off of one person!

Much of the time people you target will have already heard of these products and be more apt to buy. They might have watched the sellers youtube videos or have seen their ads before online and maybe are following them on Instagram. You need to target the sellers followers or fan pages and you will get many people that are already interested or at least have heard of this persons products. Contacting the people will be the easy part, but convincing people to buy their course may not be so easy. Always answer a potential client with a question. For example if you were selling a course on how to grow your YouTube channel you might say through Instagram's DMs, "Do you want to grow your

YouTube channel to millions followers." The potential customer may say something like "how" or "absolutely." Then it is up to you to make a conversation with them about how this course is designed and how long it is. You do not want to just give them the link right away, make sure to develop a relationship with them through conversation. You will have a better chance at them even clicking the link if you make a conversation with them and develop somewhat of a relationship. If it is in your niche, definitely consider selling courses they can be a very profitable source of income.

Make sure the affiliate products or services you are selling are in the same niche as your account. When posting products or services, post content that looks the least like an actual ad. Courses are a very profitable option that easily sell. As long as the product or service is in the same niche as your account you should be fine. When it all comes down to it pick something you, yourself, are interested in and it will be easier to be creative when advertising the product or service.

In Summary

Chapter Nine

In Summary

I have shown you that Instagram is a very profitable business and that you can make a lot of money even faster if you use the system that I have laid out for you. Remember to stop using the follow for follow method once you have 3,000 or more followers. Also, automate the follow for follow method so you do not go crazy following/unfollowing people all the time. When posting do not be afraid to follow new trends. Maximize your screen space by using tall content whenever possible. Videos and the multiple picture posts do best, so use them as much as possible to get the highest engagement and impressions. Using your Insights is a great way to get ahead in the Instagram game. Study your analytics for individual posts, and you can share them with people wanting to business with you, and you will be able to sell more services at a higher price. Using Social Blade is a smart idea and is a free resource that shows you analytics on your account that you otherwise could not learn through Instagram.

Always remember, the better you understand your audience, the greater your account will prosper. A post with at least one hashtag averages 12.6% more engagement than a post without, so it is definitely smart to use them. Make a set of relevant hashtags and use them for most of your posts. Remember to not use more than 30 hashtags per post. Do not overthink it, hashtags are very simple yet powerful at the same time. Remember to schedule your posts every month so you stay sane! Do not use every automation feature, you don't want to spam your account. Log into all your accounts every few days at the least. That way Instagram can sense you acting like a human and not a robot which will lead to certain shadow banning. Schedule your posts to publish at the most active times of the day so you will have the best chance of them going viral. After you automate your

Instagram, you will be relieved and ready to tackle your next goal. Price your shoutouts based on the average amount of impressions you receive per post. Make an advertisement banner displaying your prices and simple guidelines. Remember potential customers have a perceived value for your services and you need to make that as high as possible through strategic pricing and your high quality advertisement banner. Always follow up with your customer to see if there's anything you can do to make your service better. Just remember to follow these steps and you will see results.

Never sell an Instagram account below 100,000 followers. Make sure you have a high engagement rate before you try to sell your account. It can be even more profitable and faster in some cases if you buy an existing account to flip. When making an offer always start low and don't be afraid to walk away. If you change the name of the Instagram account, at the very least keep it in the same niche. Building and selling Instagram accounts is a great way to go when you want to make a lot of money in the long run. Make sure the affiliate products or services you are selling are in the same niche as your account. When posting products or services, post content that looks the least like an actual ad. Courses are a very profitable option that easily sell. As long as the product or service is in the same niche as your account, you should be fine. If you get anything out of this book remember to post at a consistent schedule of 3-4 times a day to growth hack your account.

I started Instagram as a hobby; it was a game to me to see how many followers I could get per month or week. Instagram is very profitable, and you can make a great living at it if you have patience and implement the system that I have laid out in this book. If you do business fair and honestly you will grow many great relationships that will help further yourself in the future.

www.ingramcontent.com/pod-product-compliance
Lightning Source LLC
Chambersburg PA
CBHW041205180526
45172CB00006B/1195